D1247293

AMAZING FEATS OF

BIOLOGICAL ENGINEERING

Essential Library

An Imprint of Abdo Publishing | www.abdopublishing.com

BIOLOGICAL ENGINEERING

by Melissa Abramovitz

Content Consultant

Dan Phillips
Director, Biomedical Engineering Program
Rochester Institute of Technology

www.abdopublishing.com

Published by Abdo Publishing, a division of ABDO, PO Box 398166, Minneapolis, Minnesota 55439. Copyright © 2015 by Abdo Consulting Group, Inc. International copyrights reserved in all countries. No part of this book may be reproduced in any form without written permission from the publisher. Essential Library™ is a trademark and logo of Abdo Publishing.

Printed in the United States of America, North Mankato, Minnesota
042014
092014

Cover Photos: Paul Clements/AP Images, Shutterstock Images
Interior Photos: Paul Clements/AP Images, 2; Shutterstock Images, 2, 29, 50, 87, 94, 97; Brian Kersey/AP Images, 7, 27, 37, 42; Chicago Sun-Times/Brian Jackson/AP Images, 9; Caleb Jones/AP Images, 13; Bettmann/Corbis, 17, 19, 21; Mark Gilliland/AP Images, 32; iStockphoto/Thinkstock, 40; Rex Features/AP Images, 47; Allen Breed/AP Images, 53, 59, 65; Lindsay France/Cornell/Corbis, 55; Gabridge/Custom Medical Stock Photo, 61; Najlah Feanny/Corbis, 69, 77; Red Line Editorial, 75; iStockphoto/Thinkstock, 75 (sheep icon); Jacquelyn Martin/AP Images, 81; Kyodo/AP Images, 93

Editor: Melissa York
Series Designer: Becky Daum

Library of Congress Control Number: 2014932562

Cataloging-in-Publication Data

Abramovitz, Melissa.
 Amazing feats of biological engineering / Melissa Abramovitz.
  p. cm. -- (Great achievements in engineering)
Includes index.
ISBN 978-1-62403-426-8
1. Bioengineering--Juvenile literature. 2. Biotechnology--Juvenile literature. 3. Biomedical engineering--Juvenile literature.   I. Title.
620--dc23
                                    2014932562

Cover: Cloning Dolly the sheep was a breakthrough in biological engineering.

CONTENTS

SCIENCE FICTION TO REALITY

On November 4, 2012, Zac Vawter of Washington was ready to put the world's first thought-controlled bionic leg to the ultimate test. He planned to climb 103 floors—more than 2,100 stairs—to the top of the Willis Tower in Chicago, Illinois.[1] At the time, it was the tallest skyscraper in North America. Surgeons amputated Vawter's right leg below the knee in 2009 after he was in a motorcycle accident. After that, Vawter helped bioengineers led by Dr. Levi Hargrove at the Rehabilitation Institute of Chicago (RIC) test and tweak the bionic leg for three years. Finally, the researchers were ready to

Zac Vawter climbed the Willis Tower in 2012 using a bionic leg.

unveil the amazing prosthesis to the public. Vawter would walk to the top of the Willis Tower as part of a charity event.

Vawter prepared for the event for many months at the RIC laboratory. At first, walking up and down stairs "was a little clunky and not particularly smooth," he told the *Chicago Tribune*.[2] But with his help, the bioengineers refined and tweaked the sensors, motors, belts, chains, and a computer that ran the bionic leg. Ensuring all these components worked perfectly was essential for safety. Safety is an important issue with all types of prostheses. However, with a prosthetic leg, having seamlessly operating parts is a matter of life and death. "If a bionic hand fails, a person drops a glass of water. If a bionic leg fails, a person falls down stairs," a report explains.[3]

Soon these components worked together smoothly. Vawter began practicing for the skyscraper challenge by walking up and down an escalator in a gym. By October 2012, he felt confident enough to climb stairs without holding on to the railing. The week before the November 4 event, he announced he hoped to climb the Willis Tower in an hour.

He actually made it in 45 minutes. His main job in climbing the stairs was thinking "climb stairs" and letting the bionic leg do the rest. His thoughts transmitted electric signals from his brain to nerves from his amputated leg that surgeons had rewired into his still-present hamstring muscle. Electrodes taped to the skin over these nerves picked up these signals and sent them to the computer in the bionic leg. The computer then translated the signals into commands to the motors, belts, and chains in the prosthesis to perform certain actions.

ENGINEERING INNOVATIONS

Vawter's successful climb took the idea of a thought-controlled prosthetic leg from the realm of science fiction into reality. The prototype he tested was unlikely to be available outside the RIC laboratory for several more years. But proving it worked brought hope to millions of people with amputations. Current artificial legs basically serve as walking sticks to

Vawter's climb of 2,100 stairs put extreme stress on the bionic leg.

WHERE DO BIOENGINEERS WORK?

Bioengineers work in a variety of private and public agencies, universities, and businesses. Most universities today have bioengineering and biotechnology programs. Bioengineers with master's, PhD, and MD degrees teach and do research at many of these schools. Government agencies such as the National Institutes of Health and the Department of Agriculture also employ bioengineers to do research, consult with other government departments and private businesses, and establish regulations for bioengineered products. Private biotechnology companies, hospitals, drug and medical device companies, and businesses that produce and sell bioengineered fuels, plastics, and other products also hire biological engineers.

help with balance and walking. They cannot maneuver on slopes or stairs. Biological engineers who work on prostheses realized an artificial limb would have to communicate directly with the user's brain to act like the "smart" robotic body parts in science fiction stories.

Scientists who work in the field of biological engineering, or bioengineering, develop solutions to complex problems such as this by merging engineering and biology. The National Society of Professional Engineers (NSPE) defines engineering as "the creative application of scientific principles used to plan, build, direct, guide, manage, or work on systems to maintain and improve our daily lives." Science is "knowledge based on observed facts and tested truths arranged in an orderly system that can be validated and communicated to other people."[4] Engineers are thus the critical bridge between scientific knowledge and useful products.

There are many different types of engineers. NSPE lists 19 major branches of engineering, and each branch has many sub-branches. Engineers plan, design, and build products ranging from computers to rocket ships to plastics to new life-forms and many others. Biological engineering is one of the main branches of engineering that contains many sub-branches. All these sub-branches relate to biology—the science of living organisms. Biological engineers design and create a wide variety of products and tools that come from, help, or otherwise relate to living creatures.

These innovations do not happen overnight. Each major project involves breaking the task into many small steps. Then, the engineers put the solutions for each step together into an integrated whole. Sometimes a critical breakthrough in one of these steps turns out to be the key that unlocks the solution to the problem. For example, the key to developing mind-controlled prostheses involved finding a way to connect an individual's nervous system to an artificial limb. The man who solved this problem was bioengineer and surgeon Dr. Todd Kuiken of the RIC. Kuiken developed a technique called targeted muscle reinnervation (TMR).

TMR rewires nerves that once controlled an amputated limb to control still-existing muscles.

TMR paved the way for allowing people's thoughts to control prostheses. Each step in this process required years of work and collaboration between many types of bioengineers and computer experts. But each step, starting with Kuiken's TMR technique, brought the idea of thought-controlled bionic limbs closer to reality.

BIOENGINEERING AND SCIENCE FICTION

Many other amazing advances in biological engineering have also transformed what was once science fiction into reality. In 1932, for example, author Aldous Huxley wrote in his science-fiction novel *Brave New World* that scientists could create different types of children by manipulating genes in embryos. Today, genetic engineering allows scientists to insert genes in or take them out of chromosomes. This technique is often used to create animals or bacteria that produce certain drugs, fuel, or plastics. The technique can also be used to create offspring with certain traits.

Another fictional idea was featured in the *Star Trek* television series. The "replicator" could fabricate food, weapons, and tools based on instructions contained in a computer. Today, scientists are experimenting

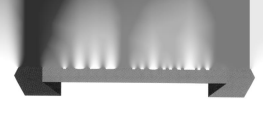

Dr. Todd Kuiken has enjoyed turning his dreams into reality since he was a child. As a boy, he designed and built tree houses and Soap Box Derby cars. As a teenager, he built his own bright orange convertible from spare Volkswagen parts. In graduate school, he built a leg brace that let him get around while carrying books after he broke his foot and was on crutches. It was natural for Kuiken to earn degrees in biomedical engineering and medicine and to later create innovative bionic limbs.

The idea of inventing a technique like TMR began growing in Kuiken's mind when he read a medical journal article in 1985. The article suggested doctors might be able to control artificial limbs by planting nerves in various places in a person's body.

Kuiken knows not everything is possible. The human body, he says in a *Bloomberg Businessweek* article, "is the most incredible machine in the world. We cannot match this."[5] However, he continues to dream up new ways of making bionic body parts better and better.

Jesse Sullivan and Claudia Mitch demonstrate their bionic arms at a press ev with the developer, Dr. Kuike

THE BABY AND THE PRINTER

Computer printers are not known for saving lives. But a 3-D printer helped save a baby's life in May 2013. Kaiba Gionfriddo was born with a blocked airway that made it impossible for him to breathe. Doctors said he would not survive. Fortunately, Dr. Green and Dr. Hollister were ready to try a new technology. Green took a 3-D image of Kaiba's lungs. Hollister used the image to generate a computer model of the blocked airway. He then fed the data into a 3-D printer, along with some PCL powder. PCL is a biodegradable polyester. The printer produced layers of PCL and molded them into a custom-fitted splint. Green placed the splint inside Kaiba's blocked airway to prop it open, and Kaiba began breathing normally.

with using three-dimensional (3-D) printers to create artificial organs and other products that save peoples' lives. In one dramatic case in May 2013, bioengineers led by Dr. Glenn Green and Dr. Scott Hollister at the University of Michigan used a 3-D printer and a powder called polycaprolactone (PCL) to make a custom-fitted splint that saved a dying baby's life.

The field of biological engineering is ideally suited to transform science fiction into reality because bioengineers integrate diverse areas of science and technology into their projects. Bioengineers incorporate advances in cell biology, molecular biology, chemistry, computer science, physics, and other fields into creative solutions for medical and environmental problems the world faces. Different types of biological engineers specialize in different areas, but all use a vast array of cutting-edge knowledge and tools to achieve their goals.

The tools bioengineers use range from gene sequencing machines to laboratory test tubes to huge vats holding bacteria that have been engineered to produce biofuels. The projects they undertake address issues ranging from toxic waste to diminishing oil supplies to shortages of human organs for organ transplants. Bioengineers clone animals, make artificial body parts from human cells, and create new types of foods, fuels, and plastics from plants. Some create computers from deoxyribonucleic acid (DNA) or engineer life-forms from nonliving materials. Some engineer products that mimic the way certain animals or microorganisms operate.

Bioengineers see progress and solutions emerging each day. They gain satisfaction from knowing these solutions are improving the world and are also awed because they are transforming science fiction into reality.

BIOLOGICAL ENGINEERING

The field of biological engineering officially originated during the 1900s, but the links between biology and engineering were established far earlier. Farmers were the first to use agricultural engineering to improve their crops. Farmers in Central America started planting hybrid corn seeds for this purpose at least 7,000 years ago. However, the first working links between nonplant biology and engineering did not begin forming until the 1600s.

Before the 1600s, most doctors believed supernatural forces and substances they called humours governed the workings of human and animal bodies. In 1628, the British physician William Harvey was one of

Medical knowledge greatly increased after the 1600s.

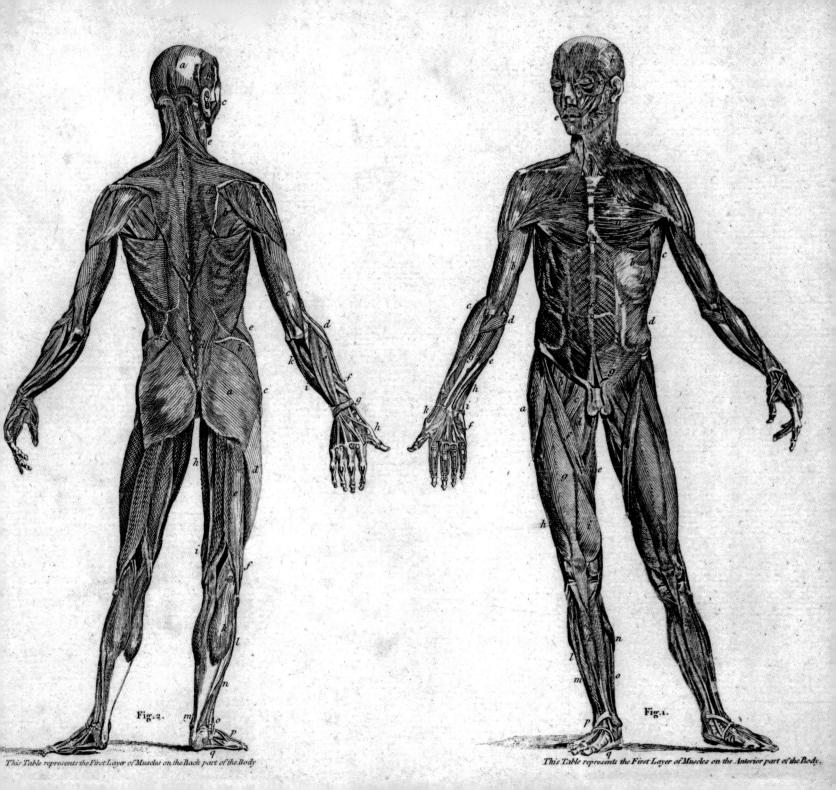

Fig. 2.

This Table represents the First Layer of Muscles on the Back part of the Body

Fig. 1.

This Table represents the First Layer of Muscles on the Anterior part of the Body.

IMHOTEP

Biology and engineering were not professionally linked until the field of bioengineering was officially established in the 1900s. It is interesting that the man historians consider to be the world's first practicing doctor was also the world's first practicing engineer. This man, Imhotep, was the Egyptian Pharaoh Zoser's court physician in approximately 2750 BCE. Imhotep also designed and supervised the building of the Step Pyramid at Saqqâra. Although he was both a physician and an engineer, historians do not know whether he mixed medicine with engineering.

the first to suggest living creatures function according to principles of physics like machines do. Harvey described the heart as a muscle that pumps blood throughout the body. Soon afterward, the French mathematician and scientist René Descartes wrote that the entire human body is run by organs that operate like nonliving machines. The realization that biology had much in common with mechanics and engineering was the first step toward merging the two disciplines. Instead of attributing behavior and illness to mysterious forces, people started to understand living organisms had working parts that could malfunction or even be fixed with certain tools.

Advances in the field of neurology also played a role in unifying biology and engineering. In the mid-1800s, neuroscientists proved that human and animal nerve cells produce electric signals that are similar to signals produced by electric circuits and wires.

Around this time, scientists also began building medical devices to improve health care. For example, physicist and physician Hermann von Helmholtz invented the ophthalmoscope that allows doctors to see into

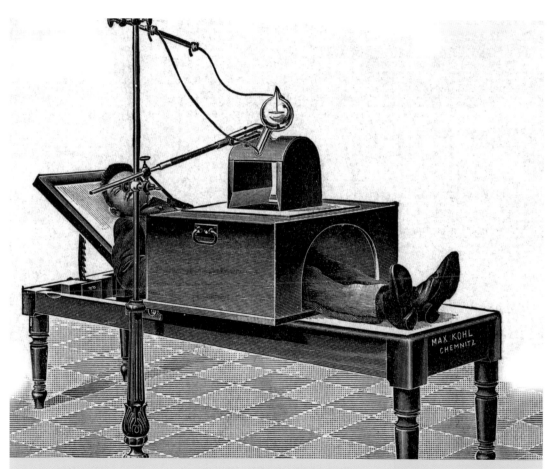

The improvement of doctors' tools, including X rays, allowed new medical discoveries and better treatment of disease.

the back of the eye, and William Roentgen invented the X ray imaging machine. Using sophisticated tools for medical diagnosis and treatment made doctors and engineers realize biology and engineering could complement each other.

ENGINEERING PROGRESS

At the same time, the separate field of engineering was also expanding beyond its traditional role in designing buildings, roads, bridges, and simple machines. During the Industrial Revolution in the 1800s, the invention of items such as the first plastics, the light bulb, and the telephone opened new areas in electrical, communications, and materials engineering. New farming tools and methods of breeding better crops broadened agricultural engineering. Historians consider modern agricultural engineering to be the first branch of the field of biological engineering.

Other advances in the physical sciences in the early to mid-1900s enhanced scientists' understanding of molecules and atoms. During this same era, the realization that physical objects shared some of the basic submicroscopic elements with living cells further unified engineering and biology. In 1953, physicist Francis Crick announced that he and geneticist James Watson had "found the secret of life" when they described the structure of DNA molecules.[1] This milestone launched the discipline of molecular biology. It tightly cemented engineering and biology together in exploring living organisms from their tiniest components to the ways in which these parts fit into a well-coordinated whole.

James Watson and Francis Crick built on the work of many scientists before them to describe DNA.

BIOENGINEERING SPECIALTIES

As biology and engineering became increasingly aligned, universities launched programs for training biological engineers and conducting research starting in the 1930s and 1940s. Many of these programs were simply called biological engineering or agricultural engineering at first. Soon some programs that emphasized medical applications were called biomedical engineering. After the British scientist Heinz Wolff first used the term *bioengineering* in 1954, some programs and departments adopted this name. Different programs evolved to specialize in different areas of bioengineering, depending on the research interests of faculty members. Public and private companies also formed to expand research and product development in different subareas of bioengineering.

The subareas of bioengineering that exist today overlap to some degree. The subarea of biotechnology encompasses a wide range of disciplines. Many scientists believe the modern field of biotechnology began in 1972 when Stanley Cohen of Stanford University and Herbert Boyer of the University of California, San Francisco, first combined DNA fragments to create a new type of bacteria. This launched the field of genetic engineering, which is a major subtype of biotechnology. Basically, biotechnology involves using living cells to make products. Today,

THE BIRTH OF BIOTECHNOLOGY

Many historians place the birth of biotechnology at a delicatessen in Honolulu, Hawaii, in 1972. Medical professor Stanley Cohen of Stanford University and biochemist Herbert Boyer of the University of California, San Francisco, were attending a scientific conference. While enjoying a snack at the deli, they talked about collaborating in their research. Cohen's work involved cloning DNA fragments in bacteria. Boyer had developed a technique for separating DNA molecules with a chemical called *Eco*RI. Combining the two lines of research led the men to later separate the DNA from two different bacteria and recombine the DNA fragments into a new type of DNA. This innovation marked the birth of genetic engineering—"a scientific achievement that later rocked the world of science," according to a *Nature* article.[2]

biotechnologists produce a vast array of useful products ranging from foods to fuels to medicines.

Biotechnology can overlap with other subareas of bioengineering such as biomedical engineering, which develops products to enhance peoples' health. It also overlaps with subareas including agricultural engineering, which develops better, easier-to-grow crops and new machines to assist in growing and harvesting these crops. Some of the other subareas of bioengineering include bioenergy production, which uses living organisms to create energy, and bioinformatics, which involves developing and using computer tools related to biology.

ISSUES IN BIOENGINEERING

Bioengineers involved in all these subareas share concerns about several issues, including cost and safety. Developing bioengineering products is incredibly expensive. For example, developing the thought-controlled bionic leg at the RIC cost more than $8 million.[3] This was mostly paid for by the US Department of Defense, which funded the research in order to improve the lives of the many wounded soldiers who sustain limb amputations. The cost of the final product is as yet unknown. High-tech thought-controlled bionic arms can sell for $50,000 to $60,000 each.[4]

Experts say the availability of high-tech machines and medical treatments such as bionic limbs is responsible for many of the dramatic increases in health-care costs over the past several decades. A report by the Hastings Center research organization states, "New or increased use of medical technology contributes 40–50 percent to annual cost increases."[5] Even though bioengineering innovations enhance and save lives, many people cannot afford to buy or use the machines and treatments. This has led to controversies over who should or should not be entitled to benefit from modern technology.

SALARY AND SATISFACTION

Even with the safety and technical challenges involved in all subfields of bioengineering, it is one of the fastest-growing job categories in the United States. Part of what makes bioengineering an attractive career is the pay. In fact, it is one of the highest-paying types of engineering jobs, with a median annual salary of $87,000.[6] Even beyond the pay is the satisfaction people derive from working in this field. As bioengineer Amy Patel explains, "A really common thing that you'll see in this industry no matter what subfield you go into is that people are really trying to better society through their work. . . . It's a really inspirational field where you can really feel like you're making a difference in the world."[7]

Concerns about safety go hand in hand with concerns about costs. One reason for the high costs of research and production of bioengineering products is that strict safety regulations exist. In the United States, the federal Food and Drug Administration (FDA) regulates and enforces the safety of food, drugs, and medical procedures and devices. Researchers and manufacturers must perform rigorous, lengthy tests to ensure these products and procedures are safe and effective. This is because the consequences of drugs or products that do not work or that do harm can be severe.

THE BIONIC LEG

The thought-controlled bionic leg Zac Vawter wore when he climbed the Willis Tower is a shining example of how bioengineers are making a difference in the world every single day. This project required years of collaboration and dedication from the many surgeons, prosthetic engineers, and computer scientists who worked on the project. The researchers had to overcome numerous hurdles to make this type of artificial limb work. These hurdles involved developing technology that allowed brain signals to be received, processed, and translated into prosthetic actions. Overcoming each

Vawter needed physical therapy to help him learn to use the bionic leg.

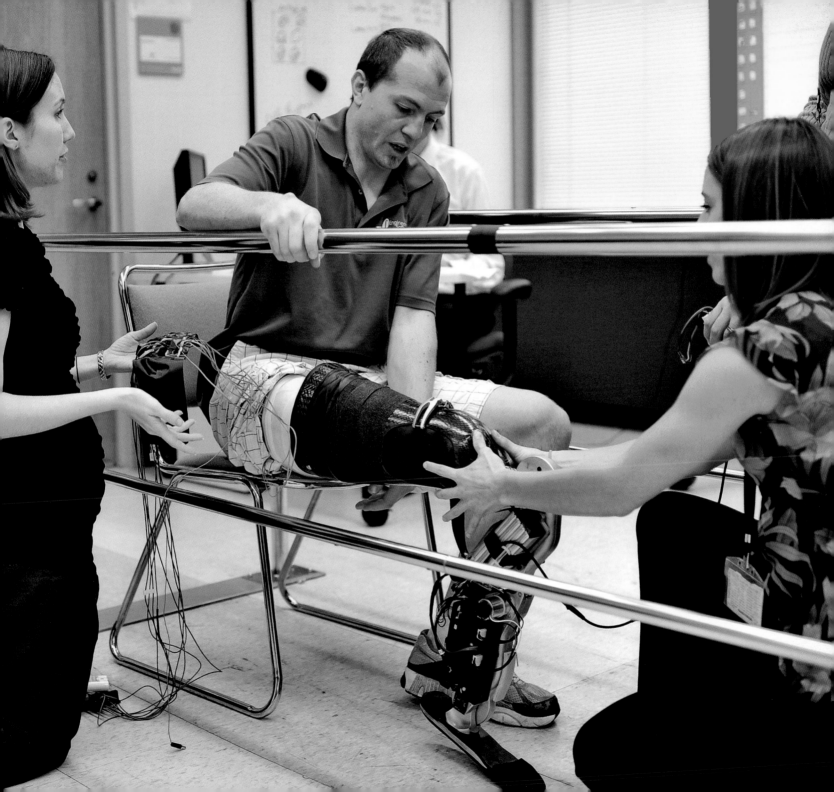

CONTROLLING A ROBOT

Most robots are controlled by preprogrammed computers that instruct them to do certain things. Others are controlled from a distance with a remote control device. However, robotic prosthetic limbs cannot be preprogrammed because it is not possible to know in advance exactly what a prosthetic user will want to do. Researchers also discovered trying to control prostheses remotely was too difficult for users.

Bioengineers devised two viable methods of controlling robotic prostheses.

Body-powered robotic prostheses are controlled by motions in other parts of the body. For example, an arm prosthesis can be controlled by the user shrugging his or her shoulders. This motion pulls on cables connected to the prosthesis' joints and makes them move.

Myoelectric prostheses are operated by sensors sending electric signals from muscles near the prosthesis to a computer. Thought-controlled artificial limbs are a type of myoelectric prosthesis.

hurdle was challenging, and integrating the solutions into a working system was even more challenging.

TMR PAVES THE WAY

Dr. Kuiken's TMR technique provided a method for hooking up a human brain to a prosthesis. The brain controls muscles by sending chemical and electric signals to neurons in the spinal cord. Spinal neurons then send signals through nerve fibers connected to certain muscles and sensory receptors. The nerve fibers that were connected to an amputated limb gradually die off because they are no longer being used. However, if these nerves are rewired into still-present muscles, they stay alive and establish connections to control these muscles. Kuiken uses a telephone analogy to explain how TMR works: "If a telephone call is unexpectedly disconnected, the caller can still speak into the phone, even if no one can hear on the other end. If the caller plugs in a new phone, the connection can be restored and the message delivered."[1]

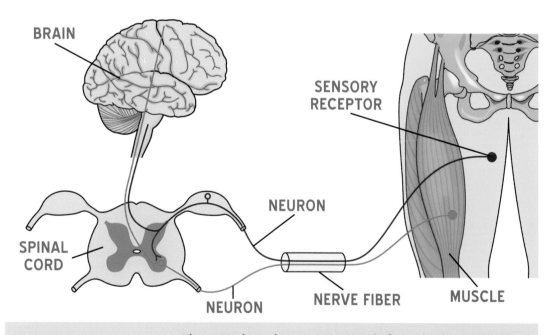

The spinal cord transmits signals from the brain to our muscles and sensory receptors.

Kuiken and his team first used TMR in 2002 on Jesse Sullivan. Sullivan worked for a power company. Both his arms had to be amputated after he accidentally touched an electric wire. The surgeons rewired what was left of the brachial plexus nerves in Sullivan's left arm to the pectoralis muscles in his chest. These nerves normally control movement in the hand, wrist, and elbow joints. After the operation, the doctors instructed Sullivan to repeatedly think about moving these joints, even though his arm no longer existed. Signals from his brain to the rewired nerves kept these nerves active, and they established connections in their new muscle home.

After approximately three months, Sullivan noticed he could feel his chest muscles twitching when he imagined moving parts of his left arm. This proved the rewiring worked; the nerves from Sullivan's lost arm were now signaling his chest muscles to move. Sullivan also reported it felt as though someone were touching various areas of his amputated left arm when they touched the skin over his chest muscles. This happened because his brain was not aware the nerves from his arm had been placed in muscles where they did not naturally belong.

THOUGHT-CONTROLLED PROSTHESES

The next step involved transmitting Sullivan's thoughts about moving his arm to a computer. Doctors can measure the electric activity in muscles

JESSE SULLIVAN'S BIONIC ARM

Jesse Sullivan initially used two motor-powered prosthetic arms after his arms were amputated. Bioengineers mounted switches near his chin that he could activate by moving nearby muscles. However, operating the prostheses using the switches was slow and cumbersome. Sullivan agreed to undergo TMR on nerves from his left arm so he could try out an experimental thought-controlled bionic arm. He said the difference between his traditional prostheses and the bionic arm was like "night and day."[2] The bionic arm allowed him to easily feed and dress himself and perform household chores. After their success with testing TMR on Sullivan, the researchers went on to perform similar operations in other people with amputations.

with an electromyography (EMG) machine. Kuiken's team asked Sullivan to mentally perform more than 20 different arm movements. They used EMG data from his rewired chest muscles to identify the precise combination of nerve impulses involved in each movement. Computer software designers then used this data to create pattern recognition software that related different thought patterns to specific movements. Prosthesis engineers then incorporated this software into a computer in a bionic artificial arm. This computer translated Sullivan's thought patterns into directions for the motors and other working parts to move in certain ways.

Thought-controlled prosthetic arms became available to the public within a few years after Sullivan tried out Kuiken's prototype. These devices have improved the lives of many people with amputations. Bioengineers next hoped to develop similar prosthetic legs to help more

Jesse Sullivan's bionic arm allows him to do many activities he could not manage with a traditional prosthesis.

WALKING IS COMPLEX

One reason designing a bionic prosthetic leg is difficult is that the goal is to mimic the natural process of walking as much as possible. Walking is a complex motion. It involves the brain and spinal cord relaying messages about the size, speed, and direction of a step to muscles attached to bones and joints. These muscles respond by moving the bones and joints appropriately.

The muscles then send back signals to the brain to let it know what has just happened. The brain smoothly coordinates the next step based on the individual's existing position. Computers and mechanical sensors cannot do everything the human body does naturally. But thought-controlled bionic legs come closer to duplicating the natural process of walking than anything else has done so far.

than 1 million Americans who have lost a leg or part of a leg from injuries or disease.[3] However, building a prosthetic leg is more complicated than building a prosthetic arm, partially because of the weight a leg must support and the power it must generate.

Other challenges in designing a robotic leg involve its weight. Ten years ago, when the first bionic arms were designed, a comparable leg would have weighed approximately 300 pounds (140 kg). Since then, engineers have developed lighter-weight plastics, metals, motors, computers, and other necessary components. They used these components to build the prototype bionic leg Vawter tested. The prototype weighs ten pounds (4.5 kg) and is mostly made of aluminum, plus two motors, a rechargeable battery, numerous sensors, and a small computer.[4]

TESTING THE BIONIC LEG

After Vawter's motorcycle accident, he and his surgeon at the University of Washington determined he would be a good candidate to help the RIC researchers test the new bionic leg. Vawter's surgeon, Dr. Douglas Smith, rewired the severed nerves from Vawter's amputated ankle into his hamstring muscle. Soon the hamstring muscle started responding to Vawter's thoughts about moving his amputated leg.

Vawter began traveling to Chicago every few months for the testing process. First, the researchers used pattern recognition software to decode electric signals produced by Vawter's hamstring muscle when he thought about moving his amputated leg in different ways. Engineers then programmed the computer inside the bionic leg to recognize the patterns of electric activity and translate them into specific motor commands. One of the most innovative things about the system is that the computer learns from an individual's thought patterns and applies this learning to its directions for moving the leg.

The computer receives input from electrodes placed over the skin on Vawter's leg and from other sensors in the bionic leg, which measure how fast he is moving and how much weight he is putting on the leg. The computer then "figures out what Zac is trying to do," Hargrove says.[5]

It took three years for the researchers and their collaborators to perfect and integrate the sensors, computer software, motors, and other moving parts into a smoothly running system. When Vawter walked to the top of the Willis Tower on November 4, 2012, this proved the researchers had achieved their goals: to allow the user to seamlessly and easily change position and walk under a variety of conditions.

BIONIC MAN ZAC VAWTER

Zac Vawter is a software engineer who lives near Seattle, Washington. Married with two small children, he enjoyed running and otherwise led an active life before his leg amputation. Part of the reason he volunteered to test the thought-controlled bionic leg was the hope of regaining much of his former lifestyle when the prosthesis becomes available. Another reason was that he wanted to give other people with amputations hope. "He's giving back so much. He's taken a less than ideal situation and made the most of it and he's helping potentially millions of people," Dr. Hargrove stated.[6]

THE BIONIC FUTURE

The study about Vawter test piloting the bionic leg was not published until September 26, 2013, nearly a year after his historic skyscraper climb. The study's publication generated even more publicity than the climb inspired. Experts hailed the prototype leg's potential to improve the lives of many people with amputations. For the first time, using a prosthetic leg came close to mimicking the natural process of walking.

The bionic leg performed even better than the researchers had anticipated. As the RIC's chief executive officer Joanne Smith points out, most people will not use their bionic legs to climb 2,000 stairs at a time.

The Willis Center test proved the bionic leg could stand up to extreme conditions.

BIONIC LEGS AND THE MILITARY

The US Department of Defense funded the bionic leg project because soldiers have lost more than 1,600 limbs during the wars in Iraq and Afghanistan, and 86 percent of these amputations involved legs.[1] Throughout history, advances in prostheses have followed wars that involved large numbers of injuries. The military believes it is responsible for helping injured soldiers continue serving if they wish or else lead full lives outside of the service. Troy Turner, manager of a US Army prosthetics research center, says most injured soldiers want to continue participating in active recreational sports such as basketball, hiking, kayaking, skydiving, and others. The army's prosthetic research leaders decided to collaborate with civilian research centers including the RIC in hopes of getting lifelike prostheses to injured soldiers as quickly as possible.

The fact that the leg worked so well during Vawter's 103-story climb showed it would certainly fulfill most peoples' everyday needs, including the needs of the soldiers for whom the project was designed.

GREAT RESULTS

Vawter was thrilled by how much of an improvement the bionic leg was compared with his everyday prosthetic leg. It allowed him to walk faster than with his usual prosthesis and smoothly transition between sitting, standing, and walking on level ground, slopes, and stairs. It even allowed him to take the stairs two at a time. However, he did comment in a *Bloomberg News* article that the leg does not allow him to do everything he could do with two natural legs. He can no longer slam-dunk a basketball, for example. "It's still a prosthetic, but it's in between the leg I wear every day and prior to amputation. It's a dramatic improvement over my current prosthetic, but there is still a long way to go," he stated.[2]

Vawter said one of the nicest things about the bionic leg is that it requires him to only think about what he wants to do:

> *In my mind, it's still the same thing in terms of moving my ankle down or up, or extending my leg forward or back. It's just walk like I would normally walk. It's not special training or buttons or tricks. That's a big piece of what I think is groundbreaking and phenomenal about this work.[3]*

Vawter and the researchers are also thrilled the bionic leg drastically decreases falling. Vawter and others who use traditional robotic prosthetic legs report they fall down fairly often. This is largely because the computers that run robotic legs that cannot incorporate the user's thoughts are likely to make errors in calculating how the leg should move. These computers receive input from mechanical sensors that measure the leg's position and how much weight is being applied. Prosthetics experts have found the error rate for these traditional prostheses is 12.9 percent. Adding in EMG data from the rewired nerves in Vawter's case reduced this

error rate to 1.8 percent.[4] The researchers found most of the remaining errors resulted in very slight changes in how the bionic leg transitioned from walking on a level surface to walking on a slope or staircase. These changes were so minor Vawter rarely noticed them.

MORE WORK AHEAD

Although the bionic leg works well, the researchers and their collaborators who are preparing to manufacture the parts of the prosthesis still plan to make improvements before the device can be marketed to the public. In particular, Freedom Innovations, the company that is building the complete leg, is working to make it lighter, smaller, quieter, and even safer than it already is. One important reason the company and its collaborators

Traditional prostheses cannot adjust to different terrain or movements.

want the leg smaller and lighter is so people of many sizes can use versions of the leg once it is available to the public.

Another issue being addressed is the noisy motors in the prototype. The engineers are working to make them quieter by tweaking the moving parts. They are also working to improve the battery, which currently needs to be recharged after the user takes approximately 5,000 steps.[5] The Department of Defense hopes the developers can double the battery's life. Another issue is that the part of the prosthetic leg that attaches to the user's thigh tends to irritate the skin. The engineers are trying to make this part more comfortable.

Although the researchers and the manufacturer estimate it will be at least 2015 or later before the bionic leg is ready for the public, scientists point out that conducting and bringing this type of research to fruition takes a long time for good reasons. Safety is the highest concern, and fulfilling the safety requirements involves years of testing and retesting. The technical aspects of finding solutions to problems such as loud motors also take time to resolve. All in all, those involved with the bionic leg project are pleased they have done so much in a relatively short period of time.

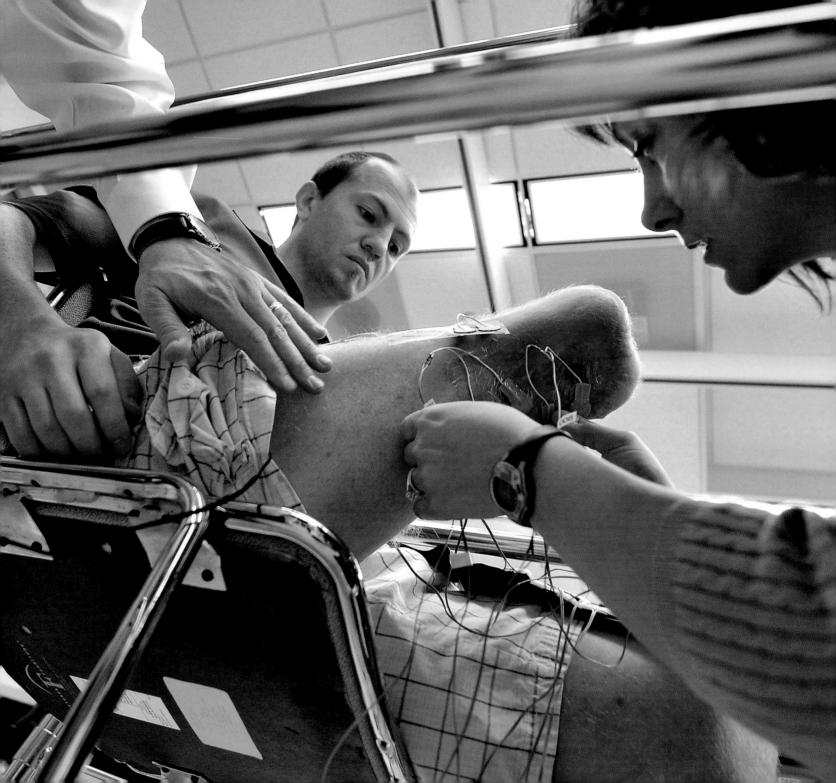

Working with Vawter and other testers helps engineers improve the comfort and usability of prostheses.

FUTURE APPLICATIONS

The technology that made the thought-controlled bionic leg possible may have other applications in the future. For example, someday it may be possible to reverse the bionic leg technology to allow an artificial limb to provide input to the user's brain. In existing bionic body parts, the brain provides input to the bionic leg through sensors and computer software. Experts believe this process could be reversed to become a two-way street in both arm and leg prosthetics. Dr. Kuiken, for instance, writes that someday a bionic prosthesis might be able to send messages to the user's brain "that will allow users to 'feel' with their artificial arm as if it were their own hand."[6]

Another potential application is that TMR technology might someday allow cars to be controlled by a person's thoughts. Hargrove believes in this scenario a bionic leg would send

REVERSING THE TECHNOLOGY

Bionic arms and legs that utilize TMR prove bioengineers can tap into the human brain and use a person's thoughts to control a prosthesis. But can a prosthesis communicate with the brain and tell it where the limb is and what it is touching? It is possible, states Dr. Hargrove in a CNET article. Hargrove explains that in order to achieve this goal, "we would need cutting-edge sensors that could perhaps be implanted in the body."[7] The sensors would have to be hooked up so they could send feedback from the prosthesis directly to the person's brain. If this could be achieved, a prosthetic user might be able to feel grass or concrete under a prosthetic foot.

AN ALTERNATIVE VIEWPOINT

Most experts consider the applications that grow out of technology such as thought-controlled prostheses to be positive advances. However, health expert David Williams believes people will be abusing this technology within 20 years. Athletes will get bionic leg or arm replacements to enhance their athletic performance.

Others will start replacing limbs and internal organs to try to make themselves immortal. As Williams argues, "If you think there's a wide divide between rich and poor today just wait until the rich find a way to use replacement parts to increase their strength and extend their lifespans."[8]

commands from the person's brain directly to the car's internal computer. The computer would then carry out the appropriate command for the car to push on a particular foot pedal. The prosthetic leg would not be involved in physically pushing the pedals.

Computer software similar to that used in translating a prosthesis user's thoughts into actions may have outside applications. In turn, innovations in other areas of bioengineering may help bioengineers design even better bionic limbs. For example, in June 2013, Chilean company Thinker Thing announced it is developing software that will interpret electric brain signals associated with certain emotions. They plan to use this technology to allow children to design and produce creative toys on a 3-D printer. This technology still needs improvement—right now it can produce only parts of toys—but the engineers working on it believe it will be feasible in the future. This type of technology, along with the technology in bionic limbs, may someday allow peoples' thoughts to command a whole range of activities.

PRINTING TOYS

Thinker Thing's chief executive officer, Bryan Salt, wants his young son and other children to be able to design and produce creative toys with a 3-D printer. So his company is using headsets that pick up electric signals from the brain, plus special software that interprets these signals when the user looks at a series of shapes on a computer. The electric signals change according to peoples' emotions. If the signals show a child responds positively to particular shapes, the computer incorporates those shapes into an imaginative toy that can be produced on a 3-D printer.

SYNTHETIC ORGANS

Other areas of biological engineering besides prosthetic engineering are achieving equally remarkable progress. The first synthetic organ transplant in 2011 represented a dramatic breakthrough in the field of regenerative medicine. This area of bioengineering involves engineering stem cells to grow into functioning tissues and organs to replace diseased ones. Stem cells are immature cells that can develop into a variety of mature cell types. They therefore have potential applications as a renewable source of cells and organs to replace those damaged in diseases such as Alzheimer's, spinal cord injury, burns, diabetes, and others. Until recently, most cell and

Dr. Alex Seifalian created the plastic scaffold for the first synthetic trachea.

THE IMMUNE SYSTEM'S JOB

The immune system's job is to fight off and destroy foreign cells, organisms, or other substances that invade the body. An organ or tissue recipient's immune system does exactly that when it recognizes an organ donor's cells as foreign. Doctors perform tissue and blood type tests on donors to find someone who is most compatible with the recipient. This is why family members who share similar genes often make the best donors. However, the immune system still rejects closely matched tissue to some degree. Thus, transplant recipients must take drugs to dampen the immune system. This can be dangerous as well, since the patient' ability to fight off germs and cancers is diminished.

organ transplants used cells and organs taken from living or deceased donors. The body's immune system rejects or destroys cells that are not its own, so organ recipients must take antirejection drugs that can have dangerous side effects. Beside this drawback, there is a severe shortage of transplantable organs. Reliable methods of making replacement organs from a patient's own stem cells have the potential to solve both the rejection and shortage problems.

WHAT ARE STEM CELLS?

The Canadian physician Ernest McCulloch and physicist James Till isolated and proved the existence of stem cells in 1961. The team was studying methods of using radiation to prepare mice for bone marrow transplants at the Ontario Cancer Institute. They discovered mice given lethal doses of radiation survived if they were injected with bone marrow cells. While investigating why this happened, they found colonies of cells that were clones of the injected bone marrow cells in the spleens of the mice. They found the colonies contained some immature cells and some specialized cells. They proved the specialized cells developed from the immature cells and the immature cells were capable of becoming a variety of cell types. These immature cells were also capable of replicating themselves. The researchers named the immature cells *stem cells*.

Researchers subsequently discovered three main types of stem cells. All can self-renew. They are unspecialized (also called undifferentiated), and they can develop into specialized cells such as brain cells, liver cells, skin cells, and so on. The type of stem cells Till and McCulloch discovered are known as adult stem cells (ASCs). Humans and animals produce ASCs throughout the body during the later stages of embryonic development and after birth. In contrast, embryonic stem cells (ESCs) are found in early embryos. The third main type of stem cells are induced pluripotent stem cells (iPSCs). These are made in a laboratory by reprogramming mature cells with chemicals called transcription factors.

THE POTENTIAL OF STEM CELLS

The three types of stem cells differ in the degree of plasticity, or potency, they possess. Potency refers to the degree to which a stem cell is unspecialized. ESCs taken from week-old embryos are pluripotent—that

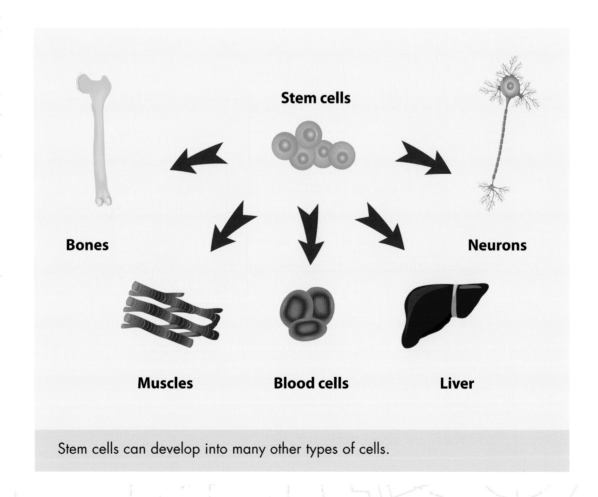

Stem cells can develop into many other types of cells.

is, they can develop into any type of body cell, from bones to organs to blood cells. After this, ESCs gradually evolve to become specialized cells. After approximately eight weeks of embryonic development, stem cells can only develop into several types of mature cells. These cells are said to be multipotent. ASCs are multipotent. Like ESCs, iPSCs are pluripotent.

Because stem cells can replicate and develop into specialized cells, researchers have devised methods of growing them in a laboratory and coaxing them to develop into certain types of mature cells. This way, they can be used to create replacement organs and tissues. However, stem cell research has been hampered by controversies related to human ESCs. Some people oppose ESC research because they believe taking stem cells from an embryo destroys a human life. According to polls, however, most Americans believe embryonic stem cell research should be allowed.[1]

Each type of stem cell offers advantages for creating different types of tissues and organs. For example, Dr. Anthony Atala of Wake Forest University uses ESCs and ASCs in engineering custom organs. He finds that using ESCs is best for engineering replacement heart tissue for patients with heart damage. This is because it would be necessary to extract a small piece of the heart to obtain ASCs, and this would endanger the patient. ASCs are useful in other procedures such as bone marrow transplants for cancer patients.

STEM CELL CONTROVERSIES

People opposed to human ESC research believe destroying embryos to obtain ESCs is equivalent to murdering a person. A document written by the US Conference of Catholic Bishops, for example, states that an embryo "has the full complement of human genes" and "is worthy of the same dignity given to all members of the human family."[2] Former president George W. Bush shared this viewpoint, and in 2001 he signed legislation that cut off most federal funding for human ESC research. Those in favor of ESC research believe early embryos are not human beings, and the potential of ESCs to save millions of lives outweighs other concerns. In line with such support, President Barack Obama signed Executive Order 13505 on March 9, 2009, to reverse the ban on ESC research funding.

ENGINEERING STEM CELLS

Bioengineers who work in regenerative medicine face several main challenges. First, stem cells must be coaxed to develop into specific mature cell types. This is called directed differentiation. Bioengineers have several methods for achieving this goal, but none are completely reliable. They can use special types of culture mediums, the nutrients in which cells are sustained in a laboratory. They can add proteins called transcription factors to turn on genes that will direct the cells to become certain cell

Regenerative medicine pioneer Anthony Atala started thinking about becoming a doctor while growing up in Coral Gables, Florida. He liked the fact that his family doctor still made house calls, and he thought it would be a good career path. He did become a doctor, but not the type that makes house calls. Instead, he custom engineers transplantable tissues and organs.

Atala earned his MD degree in 1985 from the University of Louisville School of Medicine. He began his career as a children's urology surgeon. When he began his research in the 1980s, bioengineers were just learning how to grow cells in a laboratory. Atala wanted to grow bladders from patients' cells because he thought existing treatments for some disorders were not good for his patients. He worked toward this goal for many years and finally devised a successful method of growing cells and fashioning artificial organs. He and his colleagues were the first to engineer and implant laboratory-grown organs into humans, starting in 1996. His team is now working on engineering a wide variety of organs and tissues.

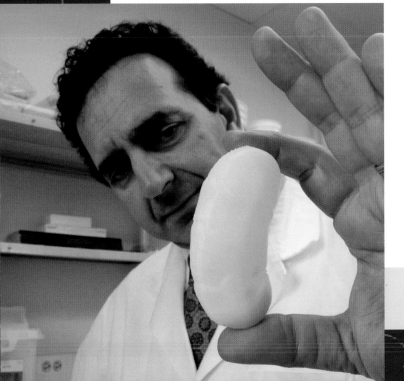

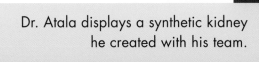
Dr. Atala displays a synthetic kidney he created with his team.

types. Another method of directing differentiation is inserting certain genes into the cells.

Another significant challenge is inducing stem cells to multiply and form together onto some sort of structure or frame that gives an artificial organ its shape. This structure is called a scaffold. Scaffolds can be made from synthetic materials or from the frame of a cadaver organ. The final challenge is placing the engineered organ in a patient's body and attaching it so it starts working properly.

In June 2011, surgeons and bioengineers led by Dr. Paolo Macchiarini at the Karolinska University Hospital in Sweden overcame these challenges when they performed the world's first synthetic organ transplant. They replaced the trachea, or windpipe, of 36-year-old Andemariam Beyene. Beyene had an inoperable golf ball–sized tumor in his windpipe. He would die without a new trachea. Macchiarini had previously performed successful transplants using partly synthetic windpipes, but this was the first with a completely synthetic organ.

BEYENE'S TRANSPLANT

Before Beyene's transplant, doctors took 3-D images of his windpipe. They sent these images to bioengineers led by Dr. Alex Seifalian at University College London. Seifalian and his team used the images to

This 3-D printer is creating the scaffold for a synthetic ear.

create a custom-fitted synthetic scaffold. They used a nanocomposite material they specifically designed to be compatible with living tissue and blood. A nanocomposite is a synthetic material made of plastic, metal, or ceramic combined with nanoparticles. Nanoparticles are tiny particles that measure between one and 100 nanometers (one nanometer is one billionth of a meter). Adding nanoparticles to another material can increase its strength, resistance to heat, and other qualities. Nanoparticles are frequently used to build rockets, airplanes, car parts, electronics, and medical devices.

The primary ingredient in the nanocomposite used to make the scaffold was silsesquioxane. Silsesquioxane consists of silicone and other elements that are not harmful to cells. It prevents tissue inflammation and blood clotting, so it is well suited for use in synthetic organs. The unique nature of this material also allows cells to attach to its tiny pores.

The London team sent the scaffold to Sweden, where Macchiarini's team soaked it in a solution containing ASCs taken from Beyene's bone marrow. The stem cells seeded themselves into the millions of tiny pores. Then the researchers placed the scaffold in a bioreactor with transcription factors to prompt the cells to grow into trachea tissue. A bioreactor is a boxlike machine that keeps a cell-and-scaffold combination at body temperature. It rotates the scaffold on a rotisserie-like device, ensuring the cells thoroughly soak into the material. After 36 hours, the synthetic trachea was ready to be transplanted. It looked like a natural trachea. The doctors removed Beyene's diseased windpipe and replaced

A UNIQUE MATERIAL

Bioengineers have used a variety of materials to create implantable synthetic medical tools such as stents, which open blocked arteries. Some materials turned out to be toxic to living cells after being in the human body for a while. Some broke down in patients' bodies. Others did not work because blood clotted around them. Patients' immune systems attacked other materials, resulting in inflammation. Dr. Seifalian's team surmounted all these problems with their unique nanocomposite material and realized it would be ideal for use in synthetic organ scaffolds. Silsesquioxane is nontoxic and does not break down or provoke inflammation. It also absorbs and inactivates a substance in the body called fibrinogen. Fibrinogen causes blood to clot to stop bleeding from an injury. Inactivating fibrinogen around a scaffold prevents blood from clotting around it.

it with the synthetic one. One of the most significant things about this groundbreaking procedure, according to Macchiarini, is that the bioengineers were able to produce a custom-made windpipe in only a few days.

CUSTOM ORGANS FOR ALL?

After the synthetic trachea transplant, Beyene spent a month in the Karolinska hospital and another month in a rehabilitation facility in Iceland recovering. He was living in Iceland prior to the transplant while attending school to earn a degree in geophysics. After his rehabilitation, he was able to go back to school. He could breathe normally and was cancer-free.

Five months after the transplant, Beyene returned to Sweden for a checkup. His doctors looked inside his trachea and reported that it looked and functioned as a windpipe is supposed to look and function. A windpipe consists mainly of rings of tough cartilage. It transports

Dr. Atala's Wake Forest University team created this scaffold for a synthetic nose in 2013.

HOOKING UP AN ORGAN

One major challenge in transplanting organs is hooking them up to the blood supply of the recipient's body. The stem cells used in the synthetic trachea transplants played a role in establishing these connections. With more complex organs, this is more difficult to achieve. A group of researchers at Stanford University are attempting to overcome this problem by growing artificial organs with attached artificial blood vessels in a laboratory. They believe this will create organs that are able to easily connect to a living blood supply.

air from the throat to the lungs. Tiny hairs called cilia in the trachea's lining and cells that produce mucus trap bacteria, dust, and other particles so these particles cannot reach and infect the lungs. The doctors observed that Beyene's windpipe was lined with the specialized cells that secrete mucus and trap particles. The organ was also fully integrated into the surrounding tissue and had developed normal blood vessels to bring its cells oxygen and nutrients.

Macchiarini and his team do not fully understand how the stem cells were able to evolve into a normal organ and to establish normal working connections. Macchiarini has suggested that perhaps the original stem cells died after the transplant. While dying, they may have released chemicals that signaled the rest of the recipient's body to send more stem cells to the new trachea to flesh it out. An alternative explanation is that after the transplant, the stem cells that seeded the scaffold may have continued to grow and differentiate into specialized trachea cells and other cells. "We are far away from understanding this process. Far, far away," Macchiarini stated in a *New York Times* article.[1]

The researchers also believe the stem cells in the new organ may have signaled Beyene's body to form blood vessel connections through

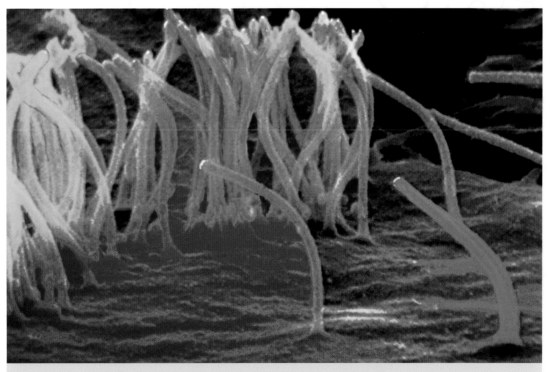

The body must generate cilia to allow a synthetic trachea to function.

a regenerative process similar to the one that caused the stem cells to form specialized cells. In effect, the researchers are relying on the body's natural response to stem cell signals to finish the job of hooking up a new organ.

More than a year after the transplant, Beyene was living a normal life. He revealed to newspaper reporters that he was happy he decided to go through with the experimental procedure. He admitted that when Macchiarini first proposed the idea of transplanting a synthetic trachea, he was skeptical: "I told him, I prefer to live three years and then die. I almost refused. It had only been done in pigs. But he convinced me in a very scientific way."[2]

LESSONS LEARNED

The Beyene transplant showed seeding a synthetic scaffold with a patient's stem cells and letting the body's natural regenerative abilities do the rest could actually work. Regenerative medicine experts believe one of the most significant benefits of this type of procedure is that it represents a huge step toward solving the organ shortage crisis. Experts also view the fact that Beyene did not need antirejection drugs as a major step forward.

ORGAN SHORTAGES

Each day, an average of 18 people in the United States die while waiting for an organ transplant. Doctors perform approximately 79 organ transplants per day.[3] In January 2014, there were approximately 120,700 people on transplant waiting lists in the United States alone.[4] People who need organs must wait for a donor who is the right size and has tissue that matches theirs closely enough. Some organs must come from a newly deceased cadaver. Others, such as kidneys, can come from living donors because people need only one kidney to stay alive. An illegal system of buying and selling organs has developed due to the severe shortages. Buying or selling organs is illegal in most places, but many desperate people pay donors to donate body parts the donors can live without.

However, doctors also cautioned that further studies are needed before synthetic organ transplants are performed routinely. For one thing, peoples' bodies can react to foreign materials—even biocompatible materials—in ways other than destroying the substance. In 2011, Dr. Alan Trounson of the California Institute for Regenerative Medicine predicted Beyene's body would likely build a wall of scar tissue around the synthetic scaffold. Trounson's prediction proved accurate. In 2012, Beyene's doctors found and removed scar tissue around the trachea. The scar tissue did no harm, but it might have eventually interfered with the windpipe's functions. The doctors do not know if scar tissue will form again.

Macchiarini and his team experimented with scaffolds made from different materials in trachea transplants they performed after Beyene's transplant. They plan to evaluate which materials lead to the least reactions. The second artificial trachea recipient was Christopher Lyles of Maryland, who also had a cancerous tumor. Bioengineers made the scaffold for Lyles' transplant with tiny fibers from a plastic called polyethylene terephthalate (PET). PET is used to make plastic soda bottles. Lyles appeared to be doing well after the surgery but died several months later for reasons unrelated to the transplant. Other patients who received tracheas made with different materials were reported to be doing well months after their transplants.

ENGINEERING OTHER ORGANS

Based on the success of the Beyene transplant, other researchers are custom engineering other body organs using techniques similar to the one Macchiarini used. Doctors previously transplanted other relatively simple synthetic organs such as bladders using other methods. In 2006, for example, Dr. Atala reported that he successfully transplanted the first laboratory-grown bladder tissues into children born with bladder defects. These synthetic, partial bladders connected to the natural bladders to mend their defects but did not replace the entire organ. The techniques

Macchiarini used with the synthetic tracheas might be suitable for total bladder replacements.

It is not too difficult to grow hollow organs such as tracheas and bladders around a scaffold. But solid organs such as hearts, livers, and kidneys are much more difficult to engineer. These organs contain dozens of different cell types and very complex blood vessel connections within and outside of the organ.

3-D printers create the scaffolds for some types of synthetic organs.

Researchers led by Dr. Francisco Fernandez-Aviles at the Gregorio Maranon Hospital in Madrid, Spain, are currently making progress in engineering a stem cell–based human heart. His team is using a scaffold taken from a cadaver heart that was cleansed of its noncartilage cells. The researchers were not sure how to direct stem cells to differentiate into the many types of cells needed in a heart and to organize these cells into a complete organ. However, the work of Dr. Doris Taylor of the University of Minnesota provided the Madrid researchers with some clues. Taylor coated a cadaver rat heart frame with rat stem cells. She placed the structure in a bioreactor and it developed into a working heart in eight days. The scaffold itself directed the stem cells to form and organize the correct types of cells needed for the heart to beat, conduct electric signals, and make blood vessels. Taylor told the *Wall Street Journal* the cells "organized themselves in a way I didn't believe. It's amazing that the [natural scaffold] can be as instructional as it is."[5] Although this type of organ might be rejected by a transplant recipient's body because it contains donor tissue, this finding is a significant step toward engineering complex organs.

CHALLENGES AHEAD

Bioengineers still have much research to do before laboratory-engineered organs of all types can help large numbers of people. Researchers must determine what makes up an ideal synthetic scaffold. They must find efficient methods of coaxing stem cells to differentiate into certain cell types.

Researchers also hope to find ways of making the cost of producing and transplanting synthetic organs affordable. The cost for each trachea transplant, for example, was approximately $500,000.[6] The day when custom-made replacement organs are available to all is still in the future. But the first successful synthetic organ transplant brought it closer to the present.

GROWING NEW ORGANS

Dr. Macchiarini believes the costs of engineering and transplanting artificial organs will diminish if he or other bioengineers can develop methods that do not require an external bioreactor. Instead, they would rely on the human body to serve as a bioreactor for the entire process. Surgeons would implant a scaffold into a patient and administer drugs to stimulate stem cells to migrate toward and flesh out the scaffold. If this technique works, Macchiarini envisions the next step as developing drugs that stimulate the body to regenerate its own scaffold and flesh it out with stem cells. Such innovations are still far in the future.

HELLO, DOLLY

While some bioengineers are busy creating synthetic replacement organs, others are creating entire organisms through cloning. On July 5, 1996, Dolly the cloned sheep was born at the Roslin Institute in Scotland. The researchers who created her named her Dolly in honor of singer Dolly Parton. According to a *BBC News* article, "The sheep's birth has been heralded as one of the most significant scientific breakthroughs of the decade."[1] Dolly was the first mammal to be cloned from a mature cell rather than from a stem cell.

Dolly the sheep's cloning was an important scientific advancement.

THE PATH TO CLONING

In 1903, American botanist Herbert John Webber coined the term *clone* to describe an organism that is genetically identical to the plant or animal it comes from. Clones can occur naturally or be engineered by people. Plant clones often grow naturally from seeds that fall off trees or other plants. Some animals, such as bees, ants, lizards, and crustaceans, can reproduce by cloning. Other animals and humans that reproduce sexually can produce clones naturally when a fertilized egg breaks into two or more identical parts. This leads to the birth of identical twins, triplets, or other multiple organisms.

People have been cloning plants for centuries by growing pieces of a plant that develop into identical clones of the original plant. But it was not until 1902 that scientists began creating animal clones in a laboratory. The German embryologist Hans Spemann is considered to be the "father of cloning" because he was the first to artificially create twin animals. Spemann tied a single strand of his baby daughter's hair between the two cells of a two-celled salamander embryo. The two cells separated and each developed into an identical, complete salamander.

In 1938, Spemann proposed an idea for what he called a "fantastical" experiment.[2] He suggested that scientists sometime in the future could remove the nucleus of an unfertilized egg and replace it with the nucleus of a mature cell. He believed this experiment might result in the development of a clone of the animal from which the mature cell was taken, but he lacked the technology to try this experiment.

In 1952, Robert Briggs and Thomas King of the Institute for Cancer Research in Philadelphia, Pennsylvania, were the first scientists to use Spemann's nuclear transfer idea to create a cloned animal. Briggs and King developed a method of removing the nucleus from frog egg cells and replacing it with the nucleus from frog embryo cells. Removing a cell nucleus is called enucleating. The researchers found that embryonic cells (later known as stem cells) placed inside enucleated eggs cells could develop into frog embryos. This technique led to methods of cloning insects, fish, amphibians, and mammals.

SOMATIC CELL NUCLEAR TRANSFER

Later, in 1962, the British biologist Sir John Gurdon cloned tadpoles by placing mature frog cell nuclei—not stem cells—into enucleated egg cells. This technique is called somatic cell nuclear transfer (SCNT). A somatic cell is a mature living cell other than a reproductive (egg or sperm) cell. Gurdon found that SCNT led the egg cells to reprogram the mature cells. This showed that it was possible to reprogram mature cell nuclei to act like fertilized egg cell nuclei. The mature cells thus became undifferentiated like stem cells are. Prompted by the egg cells, the reprogrammed cells developed into embryos and hatched as tadpoles. However, the tadpoles did not develop into adult frogs.

Researchers refined the SCNT technique to allow reprogrammed somatic cells to fully develop into mature amphibians. However, cloning animals from mature cells is less efficient than cloning them from ESCs. Scientists persisted in perfecting methods of using mature cells for this purpose because these cells are much more abundant and more easily obtained than stem cells are. They did not succeed in cloning a mammal using SCNT until Ian Wilmut and his colleagues at the Roslin Institute cloned Dolly. Wilmut began experimenting with cloning in the 1990s.

The first step in cloning Dolly was to take udder cells from a six-year-old white Finn Dorset sheep. In 1996, the researchers placed

WAS PUTTING CELLS TO SLEEP THE SECRET?

Ian Wilmut and his team introduced the serum starvation technique to put somatic cells into a resting state. They and many other experts believed this new innovation was the secret to their success in cloning Dolly. However, experiments after Dolly's birth showed putting the cells to sleep might not have mattered. An experiment performed in 1998 by biologist Jose Cibelli without using serum starvation resulted in cloned calves. Other studies demonstrated similar results. Thus, bioengineers believe perhaps using udder cells in cloning Dolly was the key to Wilmut's success. Subsequent studies have shown that using certain types of cells produces the best cloning results. Other factors that are not yet understood may have also been responsible.

these cells in test tubes to keep them alive. At this point, they introduced a new step into the SCNT procedure. They believed part of the reason SCNT rarely resulted in fully developed clones was that the DNA from the somatic cell was being damaged during the transfer process. The step they introduced was designed to reduce the chances of damage. They put the udder cells into a resting state and stopped their growth while still keeping them alive. This involved using a technique called serum starvation. The researchers cultured the cells in chemicals that kept them alive but did not provide nourishment that allowed them to grow.

CREATING A CLONE

The team then obtained egg cells from Scottish Blackface ewes and placed them under a microscope. They took out the cell nuclei with a glass needle. Then they removed the nuclei from the udder cells and injected these nuclei into the enucleated egg cells. The two cells were fused by administering a mild electric shock.

The researchers hoped the electric jolt would trigger the formation of embryos. Of the 277 cells they fused, 29 started developing into embryos.[3] The percentage of fused cells that develop into embryos is very small. This is one of the things that makes cloning animals difficult. The percentage that continue developing and survive after birth is even smaller. Wilmut and his team implanted the 29 embryos into 13 surrogate Scottish Blackface ewes' wombs. Sixty-two percent of the embryos died at some stage of embryonic development, and several others died immediately after birth.[4] Only Dolly lived.

Technically, Dolly had three mothers: the ewe from which the udder cells were taken, the ewe that donated the unfertilized eggs, and the surrogate mother that gave birth to her. Genetically, however, she and the lambs that survived until birth were identical to the Finn Dorset ewe from whose udder the somatic cells were taken. They all looked exactly like her.

Dolly's birth was a huge milestone in scientists' ability to create life. Before this achievement, scientists believed cell maturation was a one-way process. Proving that mature cells could be engineered backward into undifferentiated cells opened new possibilities for regenerative medicine and antiaging strategies.

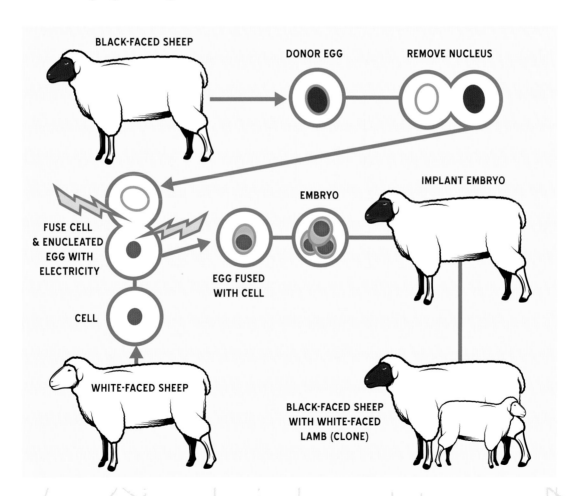

GOOD-BYE, DOLLY

After Dolly's birth, the scientists who created her kept the event secret while other scientists evaluated the research paper the Roslin team wrote about the project. The study was published in the scientific journal *Nature* on February 27, 1997. After that, Dolly and Wilmut became worldwide celebrities. Dolly was photographed and featured in newspapers, magazines, and other media. Her story inspired operas, plays, cartoons, and games. She met politicians, actors, and prominent scientists. Wilmut revealed Dolly seemed to know she was somehow special and behaved like a diva. Most sheep are shy around people, but Dolly loved posing for photographers in her barn.

Dolly with her creator, Ian Wilmut

Except for being so famous, Dolly lived a fairly typical sheep's life for her first five years. She mated with a male sheep named David and gave birth to a total of six lambs. But then she started limping. Veterinarians discovered she had arthritis. Then she developed breathing problems. Tests revealed she had a type of cancer called pulmonary adenomatosis. Veterinarians euthanized her on February 14, 2003, for humane reasons. Her body was preserved and is on display at the National Museum of Scotland.

DOES CLONING LEAD TO SICKNESS?

Dolly's death at age six raised questions about whether cloning leads to premature aging and sickness. Indeed, many cloned animals before and after Dolly have had serious medical problems. Many experts believe these problems result from damage to genes that occurs during the SCNT procedure. There are other possible explanations for Dolly's illnesses. Wilmut believes her lung disease may have resulted from her being kept in a barn most of her life. Many sheep kept in similar conditions develop similar lung diseases.

Another possible explanation for Dolly's illnesses is that she was genetically older than her five years of life when she got sick. The diseases she developed often occur in older animals. Most sheep live for 11 or

PROGRESS IN CLONING

Many cloned animals have birth defects and illnesses and die early deaths. In March 2013, researchers at the RIKEN Center for Developmental Biology in Japan announced they found a way to produce healthy cloned mice with normal life-spans. They added a chemical called trichostatin to the cell cultures in which they grew the cells. This chemical prevented the gene mutations that occur during SCNT.

Adding trichostatin also allowed the researchers to successfully reclone each mouse 25 times. Before this experiment, mammals could be recloned just two to six times.[1] The chemical was effective in preventing the cumulative genetic damage that occurred during each cloning procedure. The scientists believe this may allow animals to be cloned an infinite number of times. This could prove to be beneficial in instances where a limited number of cells exist, such as in extinct species.

12 years. But Dolly was created from a cell taken from a six-year-old ewe. The DNA that created Dolly had already aged for six years when she was born. Then the DNA aged six more years during Dolly's lifetime, so it existed for 12 years. DNA contains structures called telomeres that shorten as an animal ages. When scientists analyzed Dolly's DNA after she died, they found the telomeres were shorter than expected. However, no one knows whether her shortened telomeres caused her to age prematurely or to develop diseases.

CLONING CONTROVERSIES

Dolly's birth, illness, and death stirred up already existing controversies and created new concerns about cloning. Animal rights activists who had opposed cloning for a long time expressed anger after news of Dolly's arthritis came out. Many demanded a halt to cloning. For example, Sarah Kite of the British Union for the Abolition of Vivisection stated in a *BBC News* article,

> Scientists seem to think that they can mix and match animals' genes in a controlled way, but actually the control is an illusion. No one yet understands exactly how genes work or what the effects will be on the innocent animals who are subjected to biotechnology.[2]

Wilmut agreed health problems in clones needed to be studied carefully. But he also stated that cloning "has great potential" for technological and medical progress that should not be ignored.[3]

Other concerns about Dolly related to fears that cloning humans was not far off. Most people are opposed to cloning humans on moral and ethical grounds. Many religious groups, for example, believe creating people by unnatural means is contrary to religious teachings. They and the majority of people in general also believe cloning humans would be an assault on the dignity of the clone because he or she would be created

Activists worried about the implications and outcomes of cloning have launched protests around the world.

like a nonliving product in a factory. They worry it could be used for purposes like trying to create "perfect" people as well. In addition, many cloned animals have serious birth defects and other medical problems.

WHY DO SOME PEOPLE WANT TO CLONE HUMANS?

Some people do want to clone humans. Some want to make themselves immortal by making copies of themselves. For example, a cult that calls itself the Raelians founded the group Clonaid for this purpose. Others wish to use cloning to "bring back" a dead family member. Still others wish to clone extraordinary people. Experts believe these reasons are not legitimate. Bioethicist Dan W. Brock, for example, writes that what makes people unique is a combination of their genes and the environment in which they live. A parent who used cloning to "replace" a dead child "would not replace the child the parents had loved and lost, but rather would create a new and different child with the same genes."[4]

Many governments, along with the United Nations, have banned human cloning based on similar concerns.

Although most people oppose human reproductive cloning, many support the other type of cloning—therapeutic cloning. Both types use SCNT, but their goals are different. Reproductive cloning seeks to duplicate an entire organism. Therapeutic cloning uses SCNT only to create ESCs for use in replacing diseased cells. Some people oppose both types of cloning, and some confuse the two types. Many scientists have pointed out that it is important to distinguish the two. Wilmut, for instance, opposes human reproductive cloning, but he argues, "The potential of [therapeutic] cloning to alleviate suffering . . . is so great in the medium term that I believe it would be immoral not to clone human [ESCs] for treatments."[5]

APPLICATIONS OF REPRODUCTIVE CLONING

While most people oppose human reproductive cloning, many recognize positive applications of nonhuman reproductive cloning. Reproductive cloning is used to make copies of farm animals that have positive traits. Some of these clones are used for food. Some are engineered to produce proteins or drugs used in medical treatments. Other scientists clone animals to study how genes work and how genetic diseases develop. Some use clones to test methods of reprogramming genes. One application that is already being used is called pharming. Here, scientists use genetic engineering to create female farm mammals that produce specific proteins in their milk. Then they clone the

One potential application of therapeutic cloning is in making customized ESCs to replace diseased cells or organs. Since SCNT-generated stem cells would have the same genes as the somatic cell donor, his or her body would not reject the replacement cells. Research also indicates that replacement cells created from SCNT-derived ESCs last longer than those derived from embryos. For instance, twice as many SCNT-derived brain cells versus embryo-derived cells transplanted into laboratory animals with Parkinson's disease were alive for eight weeks.[6] This opens tremendous possibilities for treating or curing this type of disease.

animals so the proteins can be mass-produced. These proteins are made into drugs for humans.

A potential future application for reproductive cloning is cloning animals to preserve endangered species or bring back extinct species. In 2009, a team of French and Spanish scientists led by Jose Folch reported they cloned the now-extinct bucardo, or Pyrenean ibex, a type of goat. Fifty-seven embryos were placed into seven surrogate Spanish ibex wombs.[7] Only one bucardo was born alive, and it lived for only a few minutes. The researchers wrote, "At present it can be assumed that cloning is not a very effective way to preserve endangered species."[8]

Bioengineers have made much progress since the bucardo experiment. They now possess the technological know-how to successfully clone an extinct species using closely related species as surrogate mothers. However, scientists and ethics experts are debating whether this should be done. Some participants at a 2012 conference on the subject expressed the view that recreating recently extinct species would be a good thing since human behaviors such as hunting and destroying natural habitats are mostly responsible for these extinctions. Others argued the 1990 book and 1993 science-fiction movie *Jurassic Park* illustrated how tinkering with nature and introducing genetically engineered organisms into the world can go horribly wrong. Still another point of view was

CLONING ANCIENT SPECIES

Scientists have found well-preserved blood from a woolly mammoth in the Arctic Circle frozen at least 10,000 years ago. Some have proposed trying to clone a mammoth from the DNA, but the DNA is broken into pieces. Using these fragments, engineers reconstructed the mammoth genome and stored the information on a computer. Some believe they could someday clone a mammoth from this genome.

Other scientists are trying to create a genome for prehuman Neanderthals, based on 30,000- to 49,000-year-old DNA fragments found in Neanderthal bones. If this happens, it may be possible to clone a live Neanderthal. There is much controversy surrounding this proposal. Some scientists, such as George Church of Harvard University, believe humans could learn about evolution and human diseases by studying a Neanderthal. Most, however, believe it would not be ethical. Others point out that Neanderthals and other extinct species died off for a reason. Bringing them back might unleash unforeseen consequences.

expressed by evolutionary biologist John Wiens: "Why invest millions of dollars in bringing a handful of species back from the dead, when there are millions still waiting to be discovered, described, and protected?"[9]

FUTURE DIRECTIONS

Innovations in diverse areas of biological engineering continue to drive the growth of research and practical applications in this field. An aging population makes the need for innovation all the more clear. The US Bureau of Labor Statistics predicts bioengineering—particularly biomedical engineering—will be one of the fastest-growing job areas in this country until at least the 2020s. They predict a 27 percent growth rate between 2010 and 2022.[1]

With this growth, experts see a need for various improvements to the discipline. Bioengineer Drew Endy of Stanford University, for instance, writes that biological engineering in general is more complex than

The growth of biological engineering will include improved techniques and standards across the discipline.

other types of engineering because living creatures are so complex. He suggests the discipline could be made somewhat simpler and advance faster in the future by applying principles that are routinely used in other engineering fields. One widely used principle in nonbiological engineering is standards. For example, builders use standardized tools, nails, and mixtures of concrete to build buildings. But "the biological engineering community has yet to develop formal, widely used standards for most classes of basic biological functions," Endy writes.[2]

FUTURE APPLICATIONS

Even with the need for improvement, the field of bioengineering is seeing progress in many areas. Much of this progress is in biomedical engineering. But experts expect to see many more advances in applications that address environmental concerns in the future as well. One environmental concern is pollution and dwindling supplies of gasoline and other petroleum-based products. Plant-based fuels and products come from renewable resources such as corn and sugar, so much research is being conducted on using genetically engineered bacteria to produce these products.

For example, bacteria have been engineered to produce fibers called 1,3-Propanediol (Bio-PDO™) from corn sugar. The fabric manufacturer

Dupont built a manufacturing facility where bacteria decompose corn sugar into a broth in vats that are nine stories tall. The fiber is separated from the broth and purified for use in products such as carpets. The process uses less energy than manufacturing petroleum-based products does. Bio-PDO™ is also recyclable.

Other bioengineers are perfecting methods of converting sewage into electricity. Each day, more than 33 billion gallons (126 billion L) of wastewater are treated using bacteria at sewage treatment plants in the United States.[3] In 2003, Bruce Logan of Penn State University researched bacteria that can be used to make batteries known as microbial fuel cells (MFCs). He connected the two processes, using *Geobacter metallireducens* bacteria to break down wastewater and convert it into energy. Since then, other researchers have made progress in increasing the amount of power that can be created in this way. One person who contributed to progress in this area in 2008 was high school

COMPUTER MODELING

One problem with producing biofuels using genetically engineered microorganisms is that these organisms produce small quantities of fuel. Bioengineers have recently started using computer modeling tools to help determine how to increase this production. The computer model simulates the way in which a microorganism processes a sugar or other biochemical to produce fuel. Then the model analyzes the functions of the microorganism's genes. It tells bioengineers which genes should be changed to get the organism to process biochemicals faster.

HIGH SCHOOL STUDENT IMPROVES MFCs

High school student Timothy Chang used tools he learned about in his chemistry, biology, and engineering classes to design a new MFC that allows bacteria to grow and produce the greatest amounts of electricity. He used plexiglass, ceramic tubes, copper wire, and other materials to construct the fuel cell. He then connected it to a computer so he could analyze its electric output.

Chang put wastewater from a local wastewater facility into the MFC. He experimented with adding different types of bacteria and chemicals to see which chemicals made certain bacteria produce the most power. His results showed several types of bacteria produced the most power when the chemical iron chloride was added to the fuel cell.

student Timothy Chang of New York. Chang published a scientific paper about how to create an efficient MFC.

Another growing area of genetic engineering involves genetically modifying crops. This can produce healthier crops that are easier to grow. However, many people are concerned that genetically modified (GM) crops are dangerous for people to eat. This has made the use of GM crops extremely controversial.

SYNTHETIC BIOLOGY

In addition to manipulating genes for many purposes, bioengineers can now create synthetic genes using organic or inorganic materials. This growing subfield is known as synthetic biology. Creating an entire synthetic genome will eventually lead scientists to create new forms of life. According to bioengineer Robert Carlson, "a synthetic genome could be used to build an organism that produces fuel, or a new plastic, or a vaccine to combat the outbreak of a new infectious disease."[4] Synthetic genes can also be inserted into an organism's existing DNA to change its qualities or behaviors.

Other bioengineers want to use synthetic biology to eventually control the natural process of evolution by redesigning animals and humans. Endy, for example, states in an article in the *New Yorker*, "My guess is that our ultimate solution to the crisis of health-care costs will be to redesign ourselves so that we don't have so many problems to deal with."[5] This raises questions about who decides how to ideally redesign people or animals. Some people may consider qualities such as curly hair or having less than average intelligence to be problems that should be fixed. Others may just want to redesign a genome to prevent people from getting genetic diseases. "No scientific achievement has promised so much, and

LIVING CELLS, SYNTHETIC DNA

In 2010, researchers at the J. Craig Venter Institute proved living cells can be controlled by synthetic DNA. "The properties of the cells controlled by this assembled genome are expected to be the same as if the whole cell had been produced synthetically," the researchers write.[7] This means DNA created from nonliving materials can work the same way natural DNA does. Thus, the science-fiction notion of creating life from inorganic materials has been achieved in real life.

none has come with greater risks or clearer possibilities for deliberate abuse," states the same article.[6]

Bioethicists' reactions to a 2010 innovation by researchers at the J. Craig Venter Institute illustrate the moral minefield created by synthetic biology. These researchers were the first to insert a computer-generated synthetic bacterial genome into a living bacterial cell. This created a new type of cell controlled by the synthetic genome. After this achievement, bioethicist Arthur Caplan worried scientists could use the advance for good or bad. They could build bacteria capable of digesting oil spills or killing other bacteria that make people sick. Or, terrorists could build bacteria capable of killing millions of people.

ETHICS AND BIOENGINEERING

Similar ethical questions arise in other areas of bioengineering as well. In fact, all engineers face questions about whether the tools they are creating are safe and are being used for ethical purposes. Any type of technology can be used for good or bad. Sometimes the "goodness" or "badness" depends on personal opinion, as in the controversies over ESCs. Sometimes laws are enacted to prohibit certain types of research or scientific applications, but other times it is up to doctors, scientists, and others to decide how and when available technologies should be used.

In the future, more and more advances in bioengineering will be subject to questions like this. Catholic priest William Saunders aptly states the dilemma: "While we may have the technology 'to do' something, we do not necessarily have the moral mandate 'to do' that something."[8]

A Russian scientist collects bone marrow from a mammoth in order to extract DNA. Cloning extinct species remains controversial.

Biological engineers will continue debating whether some things that are possible should be attempted.

In many cases, decisions about whether to use technology come down to weighing advantages and drawbacks. For example, the price of corn rose significantly when bioengineers started using it to make biofuels. Social scientists pointed out this was hurting impoverished families by making food more expensive. But the advantages for the environment were important too.

Bioengineers are performing amazing feats that bring science fiction to reality every day. At the same time, bioethicists point out these engineers need to pay attention to lessons taught by science fiction. In *Jurassic Park*, cloned dinosaurs wreak havoc in the modern world. In the 1973 film *Westworld*, robots become smart enough to take over the people who built them. These tales remind engineers of all types about the importance of considering the possible consequences of innovation before moving forward.

At the same time, it is important for biological engineers to continue their quest for creative solutions to medical and environmental problems. Amazing feats of biological engineering such as the bionic leg, synthetic trachea, and Dolly the sheep would not have happened without the willingness of engineers to stretch the boundaries of what is possible.

HANDS-ON PROJECT
TESTING GM FOODS

Scientists have been producing GM crops for more than 20 years. They add or change genes to give these plants desirable characteristics. GM crops can be made to be resistant to insects, weed-killing chemicals, drought, plant diseases, and other assaults. They can also be engineered to stay fresh longer and to be more nutritious than other crops.

These crops often produce more, with less water and chemicals, than traditionally grown crops do. However, many people are concerned about the health and environmental risks GM foods might pose. Many claim GM foods cause allergies. Others are concerned about unforeseen long-term effects from tinkering with DNA. Many have called for mandatory labeling of GM foods.

Some people say GM foods taste different than other foods do. Some say they cannot tell the difference. Here is a simple experiment to test some GM foods yourself.

1. Buy three GM fruits or vegetables and three of the same types of certified organic foods. Look at the sticker found on many types of produce. If the five-digit number starts with 8, it is a GM food. If the number starts with 9, it is organic.

Some common GM foods include papayas, corn, and soybeans.

2. At home, taste the foods to see if you can tell the difference between GM and non-GM foods.

3. Set the foods on a table or shelf. Be sure all receive the same amount of light, heat, and humidity. Check them carefully each day for several days. Record any changes you see or smell and when you saw them. Look for signs of drying up, rotting, color changes, and other qualities.

4. Put the results on a spreadsheet that groups the foods according to the type of food and whether or not it is GM. Analyze the results to compare any differences.

5. This experiment will not tell you whether or not GM foods are safe. However, it will reveal whether there are obvious differences between some GM and non-GM foods. Consider whether or not these differences, plus the potential risks, outweigh the positive aspects of GM crops. Does eating GM foods bother you?

PLANNING A CAREER

Biological engineers need a strong high school background in science, math, engineering, and computer science.

↓

In college, majoring in biological, chemical, mechanical, electrical, agricultural, or computer engineering or in physics, biochemistry, or biology with experience doing hands-on research can lead to a career in biological engineering. Courses in software design, medical device design, and related subjects are also important.

↓

Many bioengineers also obtain advanced degrees in medicine, genetics, molecular biology, or bioengineering to broaden their understanding and skills in the field.

ESSENTIAL FACTS
THOUGHT-CONTROLLED BIONIC LEG

PROJECT DATES
Testing and development occurred between 2009 and 2012, when Zac Vawter tested the leg for the public. Further improvements continue.

KEY PLAYERS
Bioengineers led by Dr. Levi Hargrove at the Rehabilitation Institute of Chicago coordinated the project, figured out how the software, working parts, and human were to be integrated, and tested the bionic leg on Zac Vawter. Dr. Todd Kuiken at the RIC pioneered targeted muscle reinnervation. Dr. Douglas Smith at the University of Washington performed the TMR surgery on Zac Vawter to allow him to test the bionic leg.

KEY TOOLS AND TECHNOLOGIES
- TMR surgery makes it possible for peoples' thoughts to control an artificial limb.
- Computer software translates thoughts into prosthetic action.
- New materials allow for lightweight motors and other working parts.

THE IMPACT OF THE BIONIC LEG
For the first time, people with leg amputations will benefit from a prosthesis that comes close to mimicking the human body's natural brain-to-muscle control of movement.

ESSENTIAL FACTS
SYNTHETIC ORGAN TRANSPLANT

PROJECT DATES
The transplant occurred on June 9, 2011.

KEY PLAYERS
Dr. Paolo Macchiarini led the team that developed the technology and performed the surgery on Andemariam Beyene. Dr. Alex Seifalian designed and constructed a nanocomposite scaffold frame. Harvard Bioscience constructed the bioreactor in which the stem cell–seeded scaffold grew into a windpipe.

KEY TOOLS AND TECHNOLOGIES
- A safe synthetic scaffold allows stem cells to seed themselves and grow into functioning mature cells.

- A bioreactor allows the stem cells to develop into a functioning organ.

- A transplant procedure integrates the synthetic organ into a human body.

THE IMPACT OF THE SYNTHETIC ORGAN
This is the first time a completely synthetic organ made with a patient's own stem cells was transplanted into a human. The project showed it is possible to create a functioning artificial trachea in just a few days.

ESSENTIAL FACTS
CLONING DOLLY THE SHEEP

PROJECT DATES
Dolly the sheep was born on July 5, 1996, and died on February 14, 2003.

KEY PLAYERS
A team of researchers led by Ian Wilmut at the Roslin Institute in Scotland created the cloned sheep.

KEY TOOLS AND TECHNOLOGIES
- The team developed a new method of putting cells into a resting state so the cells could be efficiently transferred into enucleated egg cells.

- They used somatic cell nuclear transfer to place the udder cells' DNA into the enucleated egg cells.

THE IMPACT OF DOLLY THE SHEEP
Dolly was the first surviving mammal cloned from a mature cell. Her birth opened the door to many applications of cloning in agriculture and medicine.

GLOSSARY

bioenergy
Energy made from renewable biological materials.

biofuel
A fuel made from plant or animal sources.

bionic
Having electronic or mechanical parts integrated into body functions.

embryo
The earliest stage of a living organism's development.

enucleated cell
A cell from which the nucleus has been removed.

genetic engineering
The process of adding or deleting genes from a genome to change an organism or to create new forms of life.

genome
An organism's complete set of genes.

hybrid
The offspring of two animals or plants of different breeds or species.

multipotent
A stem cell that is capable of developing into most types of body cells.

neurology
The study and treatment of the nervous system (the brain, spinal cord, and other nerves).

neuron
A nerve cell.

nucleus
The center of a cell that contains its genetic material.

pharming
The use of animal clones to produce certain proteins.

pluripotent
A stem cell that is capable of developing into any type of body cell.

somatic cell
A body cell other than a reproductive cell.

stem cell
An unspecialized cell that can develop into a specialized one.

transcription factor
A chemical that prompts stem cells to develop into specialized cells.

ADDITIONAL RESOURCES

SELECTED BIBLIOGRAPHY

Church, George, and Ed Regis. *Regenesis*. New York: Basic, 2012. Print.

Hargrove, L. J., et al. "Robotic Leg Control with EMG Decoding in an Amputee with Nerve Transfers." *New England Journal of Medicine* 369.13 (2013): 1237–1242. Print.

Jungebluth, Philipp, et al. "Tracheobronchial Transplantation with a Stem-Cell-Seeded Bioartificial Nanocomposite." *Lancet* 378.9808 (10 Dec. 2011): 1997–2004. Print.

Wilmut, Ian, and Roger Highfield. *After Dolly: The Uses and Misuses of Human Cloning*. New York: Norton, 2006. Print.

Wilmut, Ian, et al. "Viable Offspring Derived from Fetal and Adult Mammalian Cells." *Nature* 385 (27 Feb. 1997): 810–813. Print.

FURTHER READINGS

Lee, Catherine Ivy. *Cool Careers in Biotechnology*. San Diego, CA: Sally Ride Science, 2010. Print.

Simpson, Kathleen. *Genetics: From DNA to Designer Dogs*. Washington, DC: National Geographic, 2008. Print.

WEBSITES

To learn more about Great Achievements in Engineering, visit **booklinks.abdopublishing.com**. These links are routinely monitored and updated to provide the most current information available.

FOR MORE INFORMATION

For more information on this subject, contact or visit the following organizations:

Biotechnology Institute

1201 Maryland Avenue SW, Suite 900

Washington, DC 20024

202-312-9269

http://www.biotechinstitute.org

Biotechnology Institute is a nonprofit national education organization that sponsors student competitions and provides learning resources.

National Institute of Biomedical Imaging and Bioengineering

9000 Rockville Pike, Building 31, Room 1C14

Bethesda, MD 20892

301-496-8859

http://www.nibib.nih.gov

NIBIB is a government institute that provides public information and sponsors bioengineering research. Its website has educational resources for students.

SOURCE NOTES

CHAPTER 1. SCIENCE FICTION TO REALITY

1. Jillian Jayde Hastings. "Washington Man First Ever to Climb Willis Tower with Bionic Limb." *Examiner.com*. Examiner, 5 Nov. 2012. Web. 3 Apr. 2014.

2. Michael Holtz. "Nerve-Connected Bionic Leg Helps Climb toward Medical History." *Chicago Tribune*. Chicago Tribune, 2 Nov. 2012. Web. 3 Apr. 2014.

3. Michelle Janaye Nealy. "Zac Vawter, Man With Bionic Leg, Climbs Willis Tower In Chicago." *Huffington Post*. Huffington Post, 5 Nov. 2012. Web. 3 Apr. 2014.

4. "Frequently Asked Questions about Engineering." *National Society of Professional Engineers*. National Society of Professional Engineers, n.d. Web. 3 Apr. 2014.

5. "Dr. Todd A. Kuiken: Bionic Sensation." *Bloomberg Businessweek*. Bloomberg, 8 Jan. 2006. Web. 3 Apr. 2014.

CHAPTER 2. BIOLOGICAL ENGINEERING

1. "The Francis Crick Papers." *Profiles in Science*. US National Library of Medicine, n.d. Web. 3 Apr. 2014.

2. Eugene Russo. "Special Report: The Birth of Biotechnology," *Nature* 421 (23 Jan. 2003): 456. Print.

3. Bryant Jordan. "DoD Funds Mind-Controlled Bionic Leg." *Military.com*. Military Advantage, 30 Sept. 2013. Web. 3 Apr. 2014.

4. "Bionic Arm Researchers Aim for $50k to $60k Price, Product Release in a Couple of Years." *CBS This Morning*. CBS News, 26 June 2013. Web. 3 Apr. 2014.

5. Daniel Callahan. "Health Care Costs and Medical Technology." *Hastings Center*. Hastings Center, 2008. Web. 3 Apr. 2014.

6. "Occupational Outlook Handbook: Biomedical Engineers." *Bureau of Labor Statistics*. US Department of Labor, 8 Jan. 2014. Web. 3 Apr. 2014.

7. Marc Luber. "Bioengineering Careers—Becoming A Biomedical Engineer." *Careers Out There*. Careers Out There, n.d. Web. 3 Apr. 2014.

CHAPTER 3. THE BIONIC LEG

1. Stephanie Yiu. "To Arms." *Northwestern*. Northwestern University, Winter 2007. Web. 3 Apr. 2014.

2. T. A. Kuiken, et al. "The Use of Targeted Muscle Reinnervation for Improved Myoelectric Prosthesis Control in a Bilateral Shoulder Disarticulation Amputee." *Rehabilitation Institute of Chicago*. Northwestern University, 2004. Web. 3 Apr. 2014.

3. Melissa Healy. "Bionic Leg Is Controlled by Brain Power." *Medical XPress*. Medical XPress, 2013. Web. 3 Apr. 2014.

4. Liz Stinson. "The Future of Prosthetics Could Be This Brain-Controlled Bionic Leg." *Wired*. Condé Nast, 15 Oct. 2013. Web. 3 Apr. 2014.

5. Barbara Mantel. "First Mind-Controlled Bionic Leg a 'Groundbreaking' Advance." *NBC News*. NBC News, 25 Sept. 2013. Web. 3 Apr. 2014.

6. "Bionic Man: Amputee Controls Artificial Leg with Thoughts." *CBS Chicago*. CBS Local Media, 25 Sept. 2013. Web. 3 Apr. 2014.

CHAPTER 4. THE BIONIC FUTURE

1. C. A. Kreuger, et al. "Ten Years at War: Comprehensive Analysis of Amputation Trends." *Journal of Trauma Acute Care Surgery* 73 (Dec. 2012): 438. Print.

2. Michelle Fay Cortez. "First Bionic Leg Allows Mind to Control Movement In Study." *Bloomberg*. Bloomberg, 25 Sept. 2013. Web. 3 Apr. 2014.

3. Ibid.

4. Levi J. Hargrove, et al. "Robotic Leg Control with EMG Decoding in an Amputee with Nerve Transfers." *The New England Journal of Medicine* 369.13 (26 Sept. 2013): 1237–1242. Print.

5. Barbara Mantel. "First Mind-Controlled Bionic Leg a 'Groundbreaking' Advance." *NBC News*. NBC News, 25 Sept. 2013. Web. 3 Apr. 2014.

6. Aimee Schultz and Todd Kuiken. "New Prospects for Prosthetics." *Helix*. Northwestern University, 20 Mar. 2009. Web. 3 Apr. 2014.

7. Nick Statt. "Bionic Limbs Will One Day Sense the Grass under Prosthetic Feet." *CNET*. CBS Interactive, 12 Oct. 2013. 3 Apr. 2014.

8. David E. Williams. "From War to Bionic Legs to Immortality." *MedCity News*. MedCity News, 1 Oct. 2013. Web. 3 Apr. 2014.

CHAPTER 5. SYNTHETIC ORGANS

1. Eve Herold. *Stem Cell Wars*. New York: Palgrave MacMillan, 2006. Print. 39.

2. Nancy Frazier O'Brien, Catholic News Service. "Embryonic Stem-Cell Research Immoral, Unnecessary, Bishops Say." *American Catholic*. American Catholic, n.d. Web. 3 Apr. 2014.

SOURCE NOTES CONTINUED

CHAPTER 6. CUSTOM ORGANS FOR ALL?

1. Henry Fountain. "A First: Organs Tailor-Made with Body's Own Cells." *New York Times*. New York Times, 15 Sept. 2012. Web. 3 Apr. 2014.

2. Ibid.

3. "Transplant Trends." *UNOS*. United Network for Organ Sharing, 25 Nov. 2013. Web. 3 Apr. 2014.

4. "National Data." *Organ Procurement and Transplantation Network*. Health Resources and Services Administration, Jan. 2014. Web. 10 Jan. 2014.

5. Gautam Naik. "Science Fiction Comes Alive as Researchers Grow Organs in Lab." *Wall Street Journal*. Wall Street Journal, 22 Mar. 2013. Web. 3 Apr. 2014.

6. Henry Fountain. "A First: Organs Tailor-Made with Body's Own Cells." *New York Times*. New York Times, 15 Sept. 2012. Web. 3 Apr. 2014.

CHAPTER 7. HELLO, DOLLY

1. "February 22, 1997: Dolly the Sheep Is Cloned." *On This Day*. BBC News, n.d. Web. 3 Apr. 2014.

2. Karen Wellner. "Hans Spemann." *The Embryo Project Encyclopedia*. Arizona Board of Regents, n.d. Web. 3 Apr. 2014.

3. "Cloning Dolly the Sheep." *Animal Research Info*. Animal Research Info, n.d. Web. 3 Apr. 2014.

4. Ted Peters and Gaymon Bennett. *Bridging Science and Religion*. London: Fortress, 2003. 97. *Google Book Search*. Web. 3 Apr. 2014.

CHAPTER 8. GOOD-BYE, DOLLY

1. "Generations of Cloned Mice With Normal Lifespans Created: 25th Generation and Counting." *Science Daily*. Science Daily, 7 Mar. 2013. Web. 3 Apr. 2014.

2. "Dolly's Arthritis Sparks Cloning Row." *BBC News*. BBC News, 4 Jan. 2002. Web. 3 Apr. 2014.

3. Ibid.

4. Dan W. Brock. "Cloning Human Beings: An Assessment of the Ethical Issues Pro and Con," in *Cloning Human Beings Volume II: Commissioned Papers*. Rockville, MD: National Bioethics Advisory Commission, 1997. *Georgetown Bioethics Research Library*. Web. 3 Apr. 2014.

5. Ian Wilmut and Roger Highfield. *After Dolly: The Uses and Misuses of Human Cloning*. New York: Norton, 2006. Print. 31.

6. Charlotte Kfoury. "Therapeutic Cloning: Promises and Issues." *McGill Journal of Medicine* 10.2 (July 2007). *PubMed*. Web. 3 Apr. 2014.

7. Carl Zimmer. "Bringing Them Back to Life." *National Geographic*. National Geographic, Apr. 2013. Web. 3 Apr. 2014.

8. J. Folch, et al, "First Birth of an Animal from an Extinct Subspecies (Capra pyrenaica pyrenaica) by Cloning." *Theriogenology* 71 (2009): 1026–1030. Print.

9. Carl Zimmer. "Bringing Them Back to Life." *National Geographic*. National Geographic, Apr. 2013. Web. 3 Apr. 2014.

CHAPTER 9. FUTURE DIRECTIONS

1. "Occupational Outlook Handbook: Biomedical Engineers." *Bureau of Labor Statistics*. US Department of Labor, 8 Jan. 2014. Web. 3 Apr. 2014.

2. Drew Endy. "Foundations for Engineering Biology." *Nature* 438 (24 Nov. 2005): 449. Print.

3. George Church and Ed Regis. *Regenesis*. New York: Basic, 2012. Print. 5.

4. Robert H. Carlson. *Biology Is Technology: The Promise, Peril, and New Business of Engineering Life*. Boston: Harvard UP, 2010. Print. 36.

5. Michael Specter. "A Life of Its Own." *New Yorker*. New Yorker, 28 Sept. 2009. Web. 3 Apr. 2014.

6. Ibid.

7. Daniel G. Gibson, et al. "Creation of a Bacterial Cell Controlled by a Chemically Synthesized Genome." *Science* 329.5987 (2 July 2010): 52–55. Print.

8. Fr. William Saunders. "Why Human Cloning Is Immoral." *Catholic Culture*. Trinity Communications, n.d. Web. 3 Apr. 2014.

INDEX

ABOUT THE AUTHOR

Melissa Abramovitz has been a freelance writer for more than 25 years and specializes in writing nonfiction magazine articles and books for all age groups. She is the author of hundreds of magazine articles, more than 30 educational books for children and teenagers, numerous poems and short stories, and several children's picture books. Her book for writers, *A Treasure Trove of Opportunity: How to Write and Sell Articles for Children's Magazines*, has been widely acclaimed since its publication in 2012. Melissa holds a degree in psychology from the University of California, San Diego and is a graduate of the Institute of Children's Literature. Visit her website at http://www.melissaabramovitz.com.